Hey, anxiety…

from fear to friendship—a personal journey

Elizabeth Bloomfield

© Elizabeth Bloomfield 2022

All rights reserved. Except for the quotation of short passages for the purposes of criticism and review, no part of this publication may be reproduced, stored in a retrieval system, or transmitted in any form or by any means, electronic, mechanical, photocopying, recording, or otherwise, without the prior written permission of the Copyright Authority Ltd. or the publisher.

ISBN: 978-1-922784-08-7

First published in Australia July 2022

Printed by Clark and Mackay, Brisbane, Australia

*To everyone who
suffers an anxiety condition,
and to all those who
love and support them.*

Contents

From the author **vii**
How to use this book **xiii**

Inspiration **1**
Hey, anxiety… **9**
Acknowledgements **69**
About the author **71**
Work/note book **73**
Closing words **90**

From the author

Anxiety disorders can be frightening, destabilising and overwhelming. Combine this toxic trio with the accompanying loss of personal power, and you have quite the emotional cocktail. To feel anxious is miserable: it saps your energy, negates your joy and hinders or paralyses your engagement with others.

Feeling anxious, for me, began early—probably at around the age of six or seven. Its associated disorders—depression, panic attacks and hypervigilance—set in over the next decade or so, culminating in a breakdown when I was twenty-two. In my mid/late twenties and on the verge of another breakdown, I was fortunate enough to find an insightful GP who referred me to a psychologist and advised me to read *You Can Heal Your Life* by Louise Hay. I devoured every word of that book and completed all the exercises at least twice! Another of Louise's books, *Heal Your Body*, very quickly became my bible.

There was so much shame attached to mental health in those days. I'd been brought up to believe that only 'lunatics'—or worse, 'self-indulgent people'—went to see 'quacks' or 'charlatans.' Decent, sane folk just got on with things and didn't make a fuss. Thank goodness we are more open minded, accepting and respectful of ourselves, and our distinguished professionals, in the current era.

My psychologist—a kind, gentle man—assured me I wasn't going mad, suggested I take time off to go out into the wilderness or become a beach bum, and gave me homework. I had to stop by the teddy bear shop on my way home (yes, there was one!) and buy the bear I fell in love with at first sight. My 'teddy bear' turned out to be a little black dog called Thomas, but he had the desired effect—how I adored that dog!

Fast-forward thirty years to 2020, during our second COVID lockdown. Most people, unless classified as handling 'Essential Services,' were staying home, going nowhere. Some were overwhelmed with problems concerning their children or finances, and others were lonely and isolated. The media was reporting that anxiety conditions were on the rise at an alarming rate, and even people who'd never knowingly experienced any form of mental illness before were becoming symptomatic.

Prior to the pandemic, I'd been practising *replacing resistance with acceptance* in my meditations and my daily life, but I still felt I was at the mercy of an unpredictable force that could unsettle me at will.

Over the years, I'd tried all kinds of therapy, including CBT, ACT, somatic therapy, talk therapy—and alternative therapies such as the Alexander technique, the Feldenkrais Method, yoga, kinesiology and craniosacral therapy. I'd drunk teas and taken remedies, seen spiritual healers and gone on fasts… *All* helped to a greater or lesser degree, but it wasn't until I started a course of EMDR (Eye Movement Desensitisation Reprocessing) that deeper shifts began to happen.

My journey with EMDR is worthy of a book by itself, but very briefly, this therapy succeeded in releasing embedded patterns of behaviour from earlier traumas, enabling me to operate from a more stable foundation.

Even then, I was still susceptible to triggers, particularly when linked to feelings of safety, and the pandemic set off a bunch of triggers!

I had always felt significant embarrassment about my anxiety and rarely shared details with others. During the pandemic, and with anxiety conditions reaching epidemic proportions, I started to feel less alone, that it wasn't just me *being weak* or *not coping*. It was, I thought, the ideal time to try something new.

I wanted to create a feeling of safety even when anxiety came to visit. So, that meant I had to work on my relationship with my anxious thoughts—I had to try to communicate with the parts of myself that I had previously pushed away.

During the self-isolation period, I decided to give myself a thirty-day challenge. Every day, I would open my journal and, keeping it casual, write *Hey, anxiety…* or *What's up, anxiety?*; I'd then wait to see if anything came into my mind. It was kind of bizarre, I grant you, but I would practice being still and open to whatever thoughts and inspirations might appear.

What follows is the journey of that month. It started very slowly, very tentatively, like the beginning of a new relationship, and then gathered more openness as the days went along. Going through this daily, repetitive process helped me greatly to lessen the hypervigilance, that feeling you get when you know anxiety is coming on and you brace, holding your breath, hands sweating, heart pounding—powerless to stop the juggernaut.

It wasn't an easy month—I was changing the patterns of a lifetime, and some days were quite brutal—but I had the support of my husband and the time to focus on rest and recovery.

The changes after that month were subtle. At first, I didn't notice much at all, but over time, I realised that my responses to familiar situations and events were much calmer than they typically would have been. I seemed to have developed 'space' in my mind and the time to respond to events in a more balanced way. Other significant differences were… feeling supported, rather than undermined; feeling part of a team, rather than being alone; and feeling more in control of my emotions. I was also able to self-regulate and talk logically to myself when triggered by an experience that catapulted me back to a sensitive memory.

There seem to be as many pathways to healing as there are folks wishing to be healed. My thirty-day experiment may not suit you, but I truly hope you find something in the following pages that resonates. The one truth I've discovered is that healing is a journey and a process—sometimes pleasant, sometimes rocky, sometimes joyful and sometimes horrible—it's just never the end! I have never reached a stage where I only have good days.

Knowing that, and accepting that, has given me a much greater feeling of personal safety and a much more enjoyable life.

Thank you for taking the time to read *Hey, anxiety…*

Sending every kind wish to you on your own healing journey,

Elizabeth

How to use this book

- Read it all the way through
- Read a little each day
- Dip into it at random or as needed
- Use it as a work/note book

Suggestions for using the work/note pages:

- Copy relevant verses
- Write your own version(s)
- Record notes or feelings
- Jot down random thoughts
- Reflect on the day
- Doodle or draw!
- Write freely, write anything!
- Compose a poem
- Come back and add to it as often as you wish
- Continue in your own journal

Inspiration

❝

We cannot selectively numb emotions. When we numb the painful emotions, we also numb the positive emotions.

—**Brené Brown,** *The Atlas of the Heart*

Start where you are,
Use what you have,
Do what you can.

—Arthur Ashe

Recovery, at least for me, hasn't been one step forward, two steps back. It's more like a step-and-a-half forward; six steps back; stumble forward a little; tip over sideways for a minute; gain quite a few steps; wait… is this the right staircase? Just. Keep. Stepping.

—Dr. Glenn Doyle

And then I realized that any important achievement is essentially a triumph over fear.

—Robin Sharma,
The Everyday Hero Manifesto

Hey, anxiety…

Shall we walk,
side by side,
through this day together?

Hey, anxiety…

I want you to know that
everything you feel is okay…

Hey, anxiety…

Let's breathe together!

Breathe in for three,
Breathe out for three…
Breathe in for three,
Breathe out for four…
Breathe in for three,
Breathe out for five…

Now, let's breathe normally…

Hey, anxiety…

Why don't we imagine we're
sitting on a riverbank?

Side by side,
Holding hands if you like,
Just watching the cool, clear water
pass us by…

Hey, anxiety…

Some days, we feel so rough.

On those days, why don't we try to keep things simple and put away our needs for perfection 'til tomorrow?

It's just one day…

There's no pressure, no pressure, no pressure…

Hello, anxiety!

Shall we get to know each other a little?

If there's anything you'd like to tell me,
I'd love to hear it…

I can wait,
so take all the time you need…

Hey, anxiety…

Do you know what makes you smile?
Do you know what makes you sad?
Is there anything concerning you right now?

Hey, anxiety…

I believe we can help each other…
I'll keep us calm while you keep us safe.
Does that sound like a plan?

Hey, anxiety…

I want you to know that I'm right here for you, no matter what…

If you need anything, please just ask…

Heya, anxiety…

You've told me that sometimes you feel we are revving at a much higher level than others; I know how exhausting that can be!

It's like having a foot on the accelerator and not being able to take it off…

Why don't we spend a little time outside today, just looking at the world around us and appreciating one thing at a time?

Whether that's a bird, a tree, a building or the sky…

Hello, anxiety…

I know we have tough days, and we just want to hide… but that, too, is okay. We can always grab our favourite blanket and curl up in its warmth…

After a while, we'll feel stronger
and capable of going on.

And let's forgive ourselves too.
We are not weak, but we do need time
to rest,
restore and renew…

Good morning, anxiety!

I need to do some chores today,
and I wondered if you'd like to come along
for the ride?

Who knows, we may even have fun!

Hello, anxiety…

How about texting a friend? I know it can be scary to reach out, but I promise you that on the other side of scary things are likely to be some of our greatest experiences…

In fact, beyond all the things that frighten us are those that ultimately make us happier and more fulfilled.

Heya, anxiety…

Shall we practise self-care today?

We could have a leisurely walk, pack a picnic, go out into the forest or drive to the beach.

If you'd prefer to be inside, we could run a warm bath, make some delicious soup, watch a favourite movie… or all three!

Hey, anxiety…

I hear you, my friend, but I have some work to do…

Is it okay if we catch up at five?

What's up, anxiety?

Let's be curious!

Do you remember when we were tiny?
We would wake up and greet each day with wonder
as if we saw all our experiences anew!

We were open and excited as each new moment
passed into the next,
seeing another adventure
to explore and enjoy…

Well, you know what?
Tiny us is still here!
Why don't we reach down and ask if they'd like to
come up and join
our little family?

Hey, my friend…

I see you, and I feel the pain,
the unspeakable pain of loneliness.

How do you explain to anyone that sometimes the most desolate place on Earth is inside your own head? This is truly the most brutal part of our condition…

Sadly, it's not until we've arrived at this place that we realise we must have been slipping for quite a while…

While trying to protect ourselves
from both real and unrealised dangers,
we have somehow lost our grip on
the world we used to love…

Hey, anxiety…

I am feeling our fatigue…
We didn't sleep last night,
with all our worries and our concerns.

I feel the numbing, too, and the despair…
but we *can* get through this;
we have done so many, many times before,
and we know from experience that
after the dark comes the light.

Let's try to be patient and super kind
to ourselves as this process unfolds.
We deserve to feel better, and we will,
I promise…

Stick with me—we can do this together.

I love you…

Good morning, anxiety!

I'd like to introduce you to an old friend.
Anxiety, meet *Love*!

Love would like to join our little family!
Together, we will be stronger and
more resilient, and we'll learn to relax
as we share the load…

The four of us together—
You, Me, Tiny us and *Love*—
will rebuild our lives, bit by bit…
It's going to be tough and it'll take real grit,
but we are well up to the task…

Together, together, together—
we'll laugh as we strive,
and we will not
give up!

Good morning, team!

Hope you slept well…

To celebrate our new co-operative,
I thought we could go out—take a break from our normal roles and just please ourselves!

We may have to barter a bit with each other—
for instance, I love coffee and *Anxiety* prefers tea…
but heck,
let's have both!

Let's treat *all* our differences as
part of the fun…

Hey there, anxiety!

I can't express how much it means to me that we are
starting to communicate so well,
that we're becoming friends…

For most of my life,
I've pushed you away.

I've blocked you… even tried to run from you.
I couldn't bear the *feeling* of you, and did everything
I could to try to escape that feeling,
even for a short while…

But, I was mistaken.
You were simply trying to protect me.

You've always highlighted the things that were
working against us,
and against our values—
I just couldn't see it…

Dear anxiety...

I know now that my denial of you
has caused us greater suffering...
but I'd like to share a little of what I've learnt,
if that's okay?

The 'space' where you've been spending most of your time is called the *fight-or-flight response,* and it's from this space that you've kept us safe.

I am *so* grateful that you've been
a total boss at your job!
You must have been, right?
Because here we are, still alive...

Me again, anxiety!

I also know that my resistance has

left you with no alternative but to set up
an almost permanent 'camp' in that *fight-or-flight*
space, unable to take a break or a holiday.

Actually, forget *holiday*—you haven't even had the
chance to experience the joys of being a
couch potato or a beach bum!

However, anxiety…

Happily, I'm stoked to tell you
that things have changed so much!
It's taken a while, I know,
but *now*, you can come back home
and rest…

As we begin to dismantle the *fight-or-flight* camp,
confidence and trust in each other will grow.
We will *all* be able to settle into a more balanced
and equitable life.

You will, at last, be able to sleep.

Dearest anxiety…

Safe in the knowledge that you can still do your job—
should the need arise—you'll
now be able to enjoy another
brand new relationship…

May I introduce a quality with
exceptional wisdom and kindness?

Anxiety, meet *Contentment!*

Hey, anxiety!

How're you doing?

I hope you're starting to feel more grounded as we
make our way through these brand-new days…

The techniques we've been practising do seem to be
working, especially
breathing, stillness,
walking and stretching…

Gentle routines and a morning ritual
certainly seem to suit us well!

Hey there, my friend…

It feels to me that we are slowly gathering
the tools we need,
to go—and grow—forward…

And, to leave so much of that fear
behind us…

I hope you agree?

Hey, anxiety…

Have you noticed the difference our self-care plans have been making?

Little by little, as we eat well and sleep better, everything seems to be improving!

And we're learning how to play again, coming from our new centre of calm…

Heya, anxiety...

I felt you resting today, and it made
me smile. I remember—not so long ago—
when I felt you frozen, and it terrified me.

We have come such a long way
towards understanding our own needs, and,
because of that, we're more easily able to tune
in to the needs of others...

We must be proud!

There is still work to do—there will always be work to
do—but we have started to take care of ourselves,
so our first foot is
on the ladder...

Hey, anxiety…

From here, why don't we *always*
work as a team?
I kinda like having you around!

I promise to listen whenever you sound that
high alert—then I'll investigate to
evaluate the danger of going forward.

After that, if we're sure we want to go ahead,
I may ask *Courage* to join us,
for I truly believe that the six of us—
*You, Me, Tiny us, Love,
Contentment* and *Courage*—
can do anything!

With love, and thanks, always…

Me xxx

Acknowledgements

I've been influenced by so many wonderful people along my journey. With particular regard to *Hey, anxiety…*, there are a few special people to thank.

Firstly, my husband Wayne, who has been by my side every step of the way, either holding my hand or holding me up, whichever seemed more appropriate at the time. My children, Tom and Sophie, and step-daughter, Kylie, for their love and encouragement. And to Tom's partner, Cheryl, for her invaluable support and assistance. My therapists, David Marshall and Sonia Zadro, for their patience, expertise and friendship. My editors, Lu Sexton and Leighanna Shirey. My friends, Jill, Sue S., Peter, Sally, Sue KS., Leah, and Freedy, for being there no matter what. To Abigail Gatling of Crisp Communications Co for her inspired and beautiful cover design and Jason Smith of Clark and Mackay Printers who is always such a pleasure to work with.

And special thanks to Dr. Fred Grosse, whose teachings—particularly regarding our sub-personalities—inspired and influenced me more than a decade ago. This philosophy shone a bright light for me and is at the very heart of this book.

About the author

Elizabeth was born in England into a musical family. She attended Chetham's School of Music, Manchester, was a member of the National Youth Orchestra of Great Britain and graduated from the Royal Northern College of Music as a cellist and teacher. In her late twenties, she realised she was suffering burnout from life as a musician and decided to search for another career.

In her early thirties, with two young children in tow, she started to draw while the youngest was asleep in her lap! The doodles became greeting cards and over the next few years developed into larger works on paper and canvas. Her art career spanned twenty years, three galleries and over 800 works.

These days, Elizabeth spends much of her time writing and her first book *Feel!* was published in January 2022. She also writes a blog which can be found on her website: elizabethbloomfield.net

Apart from the arts, her interests lie in all aspects of health and healing. She has always believed that emotional, mental, physical and spiritual health are intrinsically linked, and strives to highlight awareness of this in her work.

Elizabeth lives in Meanjin/Brisbane with her husband, and their grown-up children live close by.

Work/note book

Hey, anxiety…

What's up, anxiety?

Heya, anxiety!

My reflections on the book…

The best part of today was…

My tips for self-care are…

....
....
....
....
....
....
....
....
....
....
....
....
....
....
....
....
....

What's important to me?

Who improves my energy? Who do I feel good around?

....
....
....
....
....
....
....
....
....
....
....
....
....
....
....

Who or what makes me smile?

....
....
....
....
....
....
....
....
....
....
....
....
....
....
....
....

What would I like to do this year?

....
....
....
....
....
....
....
....
....
....
....
....
....
....
....
....

If I had to pick one, it would be…

If self-compassion was a recipe, what would be my ingredients?

- Two large hugs
- A generous pinch of love
- A kind word…
- ……………………………………………………
- ……………………………………………………
- ……………………………………………………
- ……………………………………………………
- ……………………………………………………
- ……………………………………………………
- ……………………………………………………
- ……………………………………………………
- ……………………………………………………
- ……………………………………………………
- ……………………………………………………
- ……………………………………………………

What, if anything, has changed about me from doing these exercises? What can I take forward?

....
....
....
....
....
....
....
....
....
....
....
....
....
....
....
....

My notes...

My notes...

My notes...

Closing words

>

Do not worry that your life is turning
upside down. How do you know that the side you are
used to is better than the one to come?

The wound is the place where the light enters you.

When I run after what I think I want,
my days are a furnace of stress and anxiety;
if I sit in my own place of patience,
what I need flows to me, and without pain.

—**Rumi**

Printed by Libri Plureos GmbH in Hamburg, Germany